What Every Manager Should Know About Big Data and Data Science

Noreen Burlingame, Lars Nielsen and Robert Masters

2016
New Street Communications, LLC
Wickford, RI

newstreetcommunications.com

Published March 2016
NEW STREET COMMUNICATIONS, LLC
Wickford, Rhode Island

Contents

Preface

What Every Manager Should Know About Big Data and Data Science is designed as a "first-book" for novices (especially managers with little or no background in the topic) who find themselves needing to understand the fundamentals of Big Data and Data Science in their professional life.

Most importantly, we have made it a point to include vital coverage of how to avoid common pitfalls when first introducing Data Science to the enterprise.

Our approach here is to describe each aspect of Big Data and Data Science in the most user-friendly manner possible, with an emphasis on the subtle art of introducing both to existing enterprises. Our target reader – the person we've kept in mind throughout our work – is the uninitiated reader coming to the subject anew, for the very first time.

Lars Nielsen

Noreen Burlingame

Robert Masters

$$\frac{4 \cdot M}{c_4} \quad M = \sqrt{\frac{5.16 \cdot 10}{3.86 \cdot 10^{26} W}} \quad W_0 \approx g \approx$$

$$\frac{2 \cdot \pi^5 \cdot k^4}{15 \cdot h^3 c^2} = 5.67 \cdot 10^{-8} W \, m^{-2} \quad T = \frac{h \cdot c}{16 \pi^2}$$

$$\frac{h \cdot c^6}{30720 \pi^2 G^2} K = \frac{h \cdot c^4}{30720 \pi^2 G^3} \approx 5.$$

$$2.821 \cdot k \cdot T = \frac{h \cdot c^3}{16 \pi \cdot G \cdot M} \quad \frac{2 \cdot \pi}{15}$$

$$\frac{\pi^2 k^4}{15} \cdot A \cdot T^4 = 2 \cdot \pi^2 k \sqrt{16 \pi^2}$$

The Vital Triangle:

Big Data, Data Science,

And Business Intelligence

Business Intelligence is about providing the right data at the right time to the right people so that they can take the right decisions.

- Nic Smith -

Computers are like Old Testament Gods. Lots of rules and no mercy.

- Joseph Campbell -

The need for precise, actionable, reliable, real-time Business Intelligence (BI) lies at the heart of the role of Big Data in modern commerce. In turn, the art of "Data Science" lies at the nexus of Big Data and BI, providing the essential methods by which BI can be extracted from Big Data's great black mass of constantly flowing, unstructured information.

This combination has a created a new profession: an elite and specialized class of highly-compensated professionals specially skilled at data cleaning, analysis, and visualization. We call them Data Scientists, and their evolving role in the organization is one about which managers must have a clear understanding.

As shown in *What Every Manager Should Know About Big Data and Data Science*, integrating data scientists (and the general practice of Data Science) into the organization is often a delicate process involving the redefinition of traditional roles within the enterprise as well as dealing with issues of territoriality amongst peers.

To accomplish this task, managers need a firm knowledge of the *what* and *whys* of Data Science, the specific BI needs it is uniquely positioned to service, and the processes by which it functions.

Such is the knowledge this important book provides.

"Data scientists [are] a special breed," says one industry pundit, "the only people with the experience and expertise to wrestle with the messy explosion of both digital (and dirty) data and big data tools. Data Science [has] become a specialized, in-house function, similar to today's Accounting, Legal, and IT departments. Leading universities [have established] stand-alone Data Science departments, conferring data science degrees, Bachelor's to Ph.D. ... Data scientists [are] either academics, independent consultants, or members of the corporate data science function, where they [will eventually] rise to the title of CDO (understood in leading organizations as Chief Decision Officer and by laggards as Chief Data Officer)."

This high-priesthood of data scientists will be in increasing demand, and highly-compensated. McKinsey and Company forecasts a major shortage of data science professionals over the coming years. McKinsey analysts predict that in 2018, for example, the USA will be short 1.5 million workers with the necessary deep analytical skill to mine Big Data for actionable information on which to base effective business decisions – not to mention also being short approx. 190,000 workers with the necessary data processing skills. According to Forrester research analyst James Kobielus: "[Organizations will] have to ... hire statistical modelers, text mining professionals, people who specialize in sentiment analysis." These same people must also be skilled in developing adaptive software models, data cleaning and mining, and related tasks.

As suggested above, Data Science is a multidisciplinary endeavor combining a range of skills in a variety of fields, together with *a strong talent for creative, intuitive thinking: the envisioning of new and useful data sets.*.

"I think of Data Science as a flag that was planted at the intersection of several different disciplines that have not always existed in the same place," says Hilary Mason, chief data scientist at bitly. "Statistics, computer science, domain expertise, and what I usually call 'hacking,' though I don't mean the 'evil' kind of hacking. I mean the ability to take all those statistics and computer science, mash them together and actually make something work."

Mason divides data science into two equally important functions. One half is analytics or, as she describes it, "counting things." The other half is the invention of new techniques that can draw insights from data that were not possible before. "Data Science is the combination of analytics and the development of new algorithms. You may have to invent something, but it's okay if you can answer a question just by counting. The key is making the effort to ask the questions. ... If I ask a question like 'how many clicks did this link get?' which is something we look at all the time, that's not a data science question. It's an analytics question. If I ask a question like, 'based on the previous history of links on this publisher's site, can I predict how many people from France will read this in the next three hours?,' that's more of a Data Science question."

"[Data Science] absolutely gives us a competitive advantage if we can better understand what people care about and better use the data we have to create more relevant experiences," says Aaron Batalion, chief technology officer for online shopping service LivingSocial, which uses technologies such as the Apache Hadoop data processing platform (to be discussed in a later chapter) to mine insights about customer preferences. "The days are over when you build a product once and it just works," Batalion comments. "You have to take ideas, test them, iterate them, [and] use data and analytics to understand what works and what doesn't in order to be successful. And that's how we use our big data infrastructure."

Not only LivingSocial, but also such organizations as Google, Amazon, Yahoo, Facebook and Twitter have been on the cutting edge of leveraging the new discipline of Data Science to make the most of their growing piles of user information.

But Data Science remains a science for which tools are still being invented – a science in a state of flux. "There are vexing problems slowing the growth and the practical implementation of big data technologies," writes Mike Driscoll. "For the technologies to succeed at scale, there are several fundamental capabilities they should contain, including stream processing, palatalization, indexing, data evaluation environments and visualization." And all this evolution is ongoing.

In the following chapters, we shall explore the range of special skills/disciplines involved in the practice of Data Science. We shall also explore such key software tools as Hadoop and Cassandra, and take a glimpse at some of the most innovative and successful applications of Data Science to date. Most importantly, we shall delve into the subtle art of introducing Data Science into existing legacy operations. But first, we will define the essentials of that vital raw material upon which Data Science feeds: Big Data.

What is

Big Data?

Part of the inhumanity of a computer is that, once it is competently programmed and working smoothly, it is completely honest.

\- Isaac Asimov -

"You can't have a conversation in today's business technology world without touching on the topic of Big Data," says *NetworkWorld's* Michael Friedenberg. "Simply put, it's about data sets so large – in volume, velocity and variety – that they're impossible to manage with conventional database tools. As far back as 2011, our global output of data was estimated at 1.8 zettabytes (each zettabyte equals 1 billion terabytes). Even more staggering is the widely quoted estimate that 90 percent of the data in the world was created within the past two years."

Friedenberg continues: "Behind this explosive growth in data, of course, is the world of unstructured data. At [a recent conference] Mike Lynch, executive vice president of information management and CEO of Autonomy, talked about the huge spike in the generation of unstructured data. He said the IT world is moving away from structured, machine-friendly information (managed in rows and columns) and toward the more human-friendly, unstructured data that originates from sources as varied as e-mail and social media and that includes not just words and numbers but also video, audio and images."

"Big Data means extremely scalable analytics," Forrester Research analyst James Kobielus tells *Information Age*. "It means analyzing petabytes of structured and unstructured data at high velocity. That's what everybody's talking about."

As a catch-all term, "Big Data" is pretty nebulous. As *ZDNet's* Dan Kusnetzky notes: "If one sits through the presentations from ten suppliers of technology, fifteen or so different definitions are likely to come forward. Each definition, of course, tends to support the need for that supplier's products and services. Imagine that."

Industry politics aside, here's an unbiased definition of this complex field:

Every day of the week, we create 2.5 quintillion bytes of data. This data comes from everywhere: from sensors used to gather climate information, posts to social media sites, digital pictures and videos posted online, transaction records of online purchases, and from cell phone GPS signals – to name a few. In the 11 years between 2009 and 2020, the size of the "Digital Universe" will increase 44 fold. That's a 41% increase in capacity every year. In addition, only 5% of this data being created is structured and the remaining 95% is largely unstructured, or at best semi-structured. This is Big Data.

Per a recent analysis from IBM, Big Data Big comprises three dimensions: Variety, Velocity and Volume.

re: **Variety** – Big Data extends well beyond structured data, including unstructured data of all varieties: text, audio, video, click streams, log files and more.

re: **Velocity** – Frequently time-sensitive, Big Data *must be used simultaneously* with its stream in to the enterprise in order to maximize its value.

13

re: **Volume** – Big Data comes in one size: enormous. By definition, enterprises are awash with it, easily amassing terabytes and even petabytes of information. This volume presents the most immediate hurdle for conventional IT structures. It calls for scalable storage, and a distributed approach to querying. Many companies currently hold large amounts of archived data, but not the tools to process it.

(Note: To these, IBM's Michael Schroeck adds **Veracity**. In other words, a firm's imperative to screen out spam and other data that is not useful for making business decisions.)

Per Edd Dumbill (and no, that is not a typo), program chair for the O'Reilly Strata Conference and the O'Reilly Open Source Convention, Big Data "is data that exceeds the processing capacity of conventional database systems. The data is too big, moves too fast, or doesn't fit the strictures of your database architectures. To gain value from this data, you must choose an alternative way to process it."

Dumbill continues: "The hot IT buzzword … *Big Data* has become viable as cost-effective approaches have emerged to tame the volume, velocity and variability of massive data. Within this data lie valuable patterns and information, previously hidden because of the amount of work required to extract them. To leading corporations, such as Walmart or Google, this power has been in reach for some time, but at fantastic cost. Today's commodity hardware, cloud architectures and open source software bring Big Data processing into the reach of the less well-resourced. Big Data processing is eminently feasible for even the small garage startups, who can cheaply rent server time in the cloud."

Dumbill further explains that the value of Big Data falls into two categories: analytical use, and enabling new products. "Big Data analytics can reveal insights hidden previously by data too costly to process, such as peer influence among customers, revealed by analyzing shoppers' transactions, social and geographical data. Being able to process every item of data in reasonable time removes the troublesome need for sampling and promotes an investigative approach to data, in contrast to the somewhat static nature of running predetermined reports."

Overall, Big Data is – in its raw form – utter chaos. Approximately 80% of the effort involved in dealing with this largely-unstructured data is simply cleaning it up. Per Pete Warden in his *Big Data*

Glossary: "I probably spend more time turning messy source data into something usable than I do on the rest of the data analysis process combined."

The data scientist takes the "chaos" of "messy source data" and finds within this morass the pure gold of actionable market information.

Creativity

And

Intuition

(*or* Posing the Right Question,

at the Right Time,

for the Right Data)

We have to continually be jumping off cliffs and developing our wings on the way down.

- Kurt Vonnegut -

"We live in the era of information and the trends that are hidden in the streams of data points," writes *TechNewsWorld's* Anjul Bhambhri. "Those who ask the right questions and apply the right technologies and talent are certain to crack the curious case of big data."

"Even if you have petabyes of data, you still need to know how to ask the right questions to apply it." So writes Alistair Croll, a founding partner at start-up accelerator Year One Labs and an analyst at Bitcurrent.

Croll cites the story of a friend, one which represents the classic example of a firm *not* asking the right questions with regard to Big Data: "He's a ridiculously heavy traveler, racking up hundreds of thousands of miles in the air each year. He's the kind of flier airlines dream of: loyal, well-heeled, and prone to last-minute, business-class trips. He's is exactly the kind of person an airline needs to court aggressively, one who represents a disproportionally large amount of revenues. He's an outlier of the best kind. He'd been a top-ranked passenger with United Airlines for nearly a decade, using their Mileage Plus program for everything from hotels to car rentals. And then his company was acquired. The acquiring firm had a contractual relationship with American Airlines, a competitor of United with a completely separate loyalty program. My friend's air travel on United and its partner airlines dropped to nearly nothing. He continued to book hotels in Shanghai, rent cars in Barcelona, and buy meals in Tahiti, and every one of those transactions was tied to his loyalty program with United. So the airline knew he was traveling – just not with them. Astonishingly, nobody ever called him to inquire about why he'd stopped flying with them. As a result, he's far less loyal than he was. But more importantly, United has lost a huge opportunity to try to win over a large company's business, with a passionate and motivated inside advocate."

Croll continues: "Ultimately, this is what my friend's airline example underscores. It takes an employee, deciding that the loss of high-value customers is important, to run a query of all their data and find him, and then turn that into a business advantage. Without the right questions, there really is no such thing as big data."

Per another commentator: "Apparently, business schools [are beginning to teach a skill generally] called 'data-based decision-making,' suggesting that the skill is reducible to pedagogical form. But 'asking the right question' remains more of an art than a science. It requires practice, patience, and time."

"Data analytics was once considered the purview of math, science and information-technology specialists," notes the *Wall Street Journal*. "Now barraged with data from the Web and other sources, companies want employees who can both sift through the information and help solve business problems or strategize. For example, luxury fashion company Elie Tahari Ltd. uses analytics to examine historical buying patterns and predict future clothing purchases. Northeastern pizza chain Papa Gino's Inc. uses analytics to examine the use of its loyalty program and has succeeded in boosting the average customer's online order size. As the use of analytics grows quickly, companies will need employees who understand the data. A ... study from McKinsey & Co. found that by 2018, the U.S. will face a shortage of 1.5 million managers who can use data to shape business decisions."

But as Kevin Weil, Product Lead for Revenue at Twitter, put it during a recent talk, "asking the right question is hard." Which is the best explanation of why people like Kevin are so important. (As the head of the analytics team at Twitter, Weil is tasked with building distributed infrastructure and leveraging data analysis at a massive scale to help grow the popular micro-blogging service. With millions of monthly site visitors and many more interacting through API-based third party applications, Twitter has one of the world's most varied and interesting datasets.)

"The fact is that even when the boundaries of a dataset are narrowly defined ..., " writes Stephen O'Grady, cofounder of RedMonk, "it's easy to get lost in it. The trick is no longer merely being able to aggregate and operate on data; it's knowing what to do with it. Find the people that can do that, whether they're FTE's or consultants, and you'll have your competitive advantage. To [ask and] answer the right questions, you need the right people."

Simply put: "Big Data becomes Big Intelligence (otherwise known as Business Intelligence) only when put in the hands of the right people enabled to ask the right questions at the right time, on a huge scale. Anything else risks the information becoming redundant and the BI worthless before it's even discovered." So comments industry analyst Mike Pilcher. (Note that most practitioners also insist that, along with asking the right questions, it is important to eliminating bias, and correlation from causality.)

Weil is correct that asking the right question (or questions) is not easy.

Productivity guru Tony Robbins notes that thinking is a process of asking and answering questions. He stresses the importance of asking the *right* questions to get the *right* answers and therefore the *right* results. The wrong questions lead to useless answers and no results, at least no positive results.

Leadership guru Michael Hyatt, says the same thing in his own way: "Questions are powerful tools. They can ignite hope and lead to new insights. They can also destroy hope and keep us stuck in bad assumptions. The key is to be intentional and choose our questions well."

Perhaps the better phrase than *ask the right question* is *innovate the right question*. Innovation is key. Or, to resort to a cliche: be sure to *think outside the box*. (Einstein once said that if he only had an hour to solve a specific problem and his life depended on it, he'd devote the first 55 minutes to figuring out the right question to answer.)

Effective questioners look at an existing reality (data) from multiple (new) perspectives.

"Of course, it's not just a matter of being willing to question – it's also important to know how to question," writes Warren Berger (author of *CAD Monkeys, Dinosaur Babies, and T-Shaped People: Inside the World of Design Thinking*). "Innovation is driven by questions that are original, bold, counter-intuitive, and perceptive. ... Coming up with the right question, the one that casts a familiar challenge in a new light, is an art and science in itself. It demands that the questioner be able to look at an existing reality from multiple viewpoints, including, perhaps most importantly, that of the 'naive outsider.'"

Creative questioning is linked to the capacity to tolerate not knowing, to seek out paradoxes, to withstand the temptation of early closure, and to nurture the "courage of one's own stupidity" in questioning commonly accepted assumptions.

"You don't know what you don't know," says Bain consultant and partner Rasmus Wegener, "and if you don't know, it is hard to come up with the right question. You need to be well-versed in both the business and the data." Then you have to begin to bravely ask *why* and *what*.

Why are our digital subscription renewals down 10% in Boston, but booming everywhere else, and what available data can we merge and sort creatively in order to move toward an answer? What customer-appreciation program enhancements will best serve our purpose of improving user retention, and how can we leverage customer-appreciation-points usage data to infer an answer? What trends can we expect to see in vis-a-vis bandwidth usage on our network come Superbowl Sunday? (What spike did we see last year on the same day? What percentages of the spike represented cell phones, tablets, PCs? How have the hardware demographics of our users changed in the past 365 days. And what is the most efficient, logical way to correlate this data and infer an answer?)

In sum: Move forward bravely – but rationally – into the unknown. Think on your feet. Realize fully what data is at your fingertips. Think analytically and creatively about how to leverage that combined data to learn and predict. Reach for knowledge. Go for it.

Making

Something

Out Of

Nothing

The only real valuable thing is intuition.
Albert Einstein -

*The power of Data Science is becoming a mission-critical
part of every business.*
- *InsideSales.com* CEO David Elkington -

Clay is nothing but a combination of dirt and moisture until the potter throws it on a wheel and "organizes" this chaotic disparity into a useful, cohesive object which is either serviceable or beautiful or both. A blank canvas and a collection of oil paints have little value when taken on their own, but when combined via the *hands, vision, skills,* and *technique* of a talented artist, they can add up to a priceless masterpiece. Just ask Picasso.

The same is true with data. Groups of chaotic, unstructured data taken on their own can be worse than useless. They can be a pointless drain of memory, cash, and manpower. However, when leveraged, organized, categorized, and creatively combined by skilled, intuitive data scientists, this same data can and usually does add up to invaluable, highly profitable Business Intelligence (BI).

William Rand, assistant professor of marketing decisions, operations and information technology at the University of Maryland (also director of that school's Center for Complexity in Business), states the point most clearly: "Data needs to be organized into information and then transformed into knowledge to become useful for managerial application."

The job of the data scientist then, is to extract finely-tuned insight from raw data: to gather and creatively combine resources, leverage these with data-parsing tools, impose assumptions on what kind of parsing should be applied to what classes of data, and intuit what questions might be most profitably imposed upon the data.

Intuit is a key word here. Like the vision of the potter or the vision of the artist, intuition and creative thinking are essential to the Data Science process: a key and uniquely human attribute without which the process cannot and will not succeed.

Does intuition make for infallible results? No. Per Mark Whitehorn, holder of the University of Dundee's analytics chair: "We're not in that territory. Of course, a good data scientist should be able to give you a probability – 'we think this is likely to be correct in 95% of the cases, 92% of the cases' and so on."

Despite imperfections, humans outrank computers in one key area. Computers are great for handling purely functional questions, but they are lousy at conjecturing and figuring out the "why" of data. They simply cannot do it. At least not yet. And even when artificial intelligence software is eventually developed to help machines at least begin to contemplate the "why," they will still need a great deal of manual human intuitive help. (A later chapter will look at fledgling artificial intelligence approaches and software heading us toward a place where at least *some* intuition will be possible on the part of machines.)

A minority of observers (especially those from the traditional scientific community as opposed to those from the business, social research, or marketing research communities) are deeply skeptical of Data

Science as a discipline. Furthermore, they are skeptical especially *because* of the human factor.

Matt Asnay, VP of mobile at Adobe, notes that since the role of the data scientist is to impose "the right questions" on data, this very exercise brings with it a bias which can contaminate the resulting BI. Statistician Nate Silver adds: "[Big Data] is sometimes seen as a cure-all, as computers were in the 1970s. Chris Anderson … wrote in 2008 that the sheer volume of data would obviate the need for theory, and even the scientific method. ... These views are badly mistaken. The numbers have no way of speaking for themselves. We speak for them. We imbue them with meaning [and] we may construe them in self-serving ways that are detached from their objective reality."

But this logic belies one key fact. *Not all bias is bad*.

Bias informed by experience and knowledge of the topic area being explored is our friend. Bias based on practical, pragmatic analysis of real world situations and real world information needs is our friend. Fact is, there's a subjective aspect to Data Science which does not exist in fields involving the practice pure-science – fields such as chemistry where one is looking for strictly defined and provable empirical results.

The *informed* and rational bias of of the data scientist in the process of unearthing, combining, and imposing questions on data is not only a valid aspect of the overall equation, but a *fundamentally necessary* element of the overall equation. Bottom line: Data Science is essentially social science, and social science (although based on empirical, statistical research) is largely subjective.

The "proof" of the value of Data Science is in the undeniable results seen by many firms. A rigorous *Harvard Business Review* study has determined that the more companies characterize themselves as "data driven," the better their performance in purely objective measures such as operational and financial results, not to mention stock price appreciation. Per the study: "Companies in the top third of their industry in the use of data-driven decision making were, on average, 5% more productive and 6% more profitable than their competitors. This performance difference remained robust after accounting for the contributions of labor, capital, purchased services, and traditional IT investment. It was statistically significant and economically important and was reflected in measurable increases in stock market valuations."

When practiced in an optimal manner, Data Science should be a maverick, revolutionary, upstart element which challenges and disrupts the assumptions of traditional business models and shines a new light on previously dark knowledge – thus creating new BI which the enterprise can and should leverage to fundamentally transform procedures, products, and profitability. This new knowledge is the "something" that comes out of "nothing" through the practice of Data Science. The ultimate program is to derive BI which informs constructive change - sometimes known as "creative destruction" – and growth within the enterprise.

As industry pundit Andrew McAfee sums up: "Data-driven decisions tend to be better decisions. Leaders will either embrace this fact or be replaced by others who do. In sector after sector, companies that figure out how to combine domain expertise with Data Science will pull away from their rivals. We can't say that all the winners will be harnessing Big Data to transform decision making. But the data tell us that's the surest bet."

Introducing
Data Science
to the Enterprise

[Data Science] infers an evolution beyond the traditional rigid output of aggregated data: business intelligence. It is a use-case-driven, iterative, and agile exploration of granular data, with the intent to derive insights and operationalize these insights into down-stream applications.
- Annika Jimenez, *Greenplum* -

There go my people. I must run and follow them. For I am their leader.
- Mohandas Gandhi -

Introducing Data Science to the enterprise often requires fundamental change in the culture of the enterprise, particularly vis-a-vis the process of decision-making and the hierarchy of decision-makers.

In the traditional corporate model with an absence of precise data, it has always made sense for firms to ultimately rely on the knowledge and intuition of the people at the "top" – the bosses – when it came time to make key, strategic decisions. This has not only been a question of rank and power, but also a reflection of the fact that the people in the upper strata of the firm have generally tended to be those with the greatest experience, the longest tenure, and therefore the most informed and viable "intuition."

Pre Big Data and pre Data Science, this was most certainly the truth. Given highly limited amounts of data (as compared to what we have available today), the top executives of a firm were indeed the people best positioned to digest that relatively small core of data and make informed assumptions. However, in the new environment where vast data is leveraged primarily for the purpose of upheaving old assumptions, the experiential (aka, "old") knowledge of senior executives is often an asset of declining (if not useless) value.

The days of the HiPPO [Highest Paid Person's Opinion] are pretty much over. Introducing this fundamental idea into the culture of an enterprise is often the biggest hurdle in creating a Data Science

initiative that is not only efficient but also has a
significant voice in the decisions derived from fresh-
breaking BI.

To be truly data driven, the enterprise must
embrace a culture wherein the very first question
asked before decisions are made is "What does the
data say?" (The shrewd executive will also be asking
key follow-up questions such as "From where was
this data derived?" and "What kinds of analyses have
been applied?" and "How confident are we in these
results?") As well, to be truly data driven, the
enterprise must include in its culture an environment
wherein top decision-makers are not only willing to
be overruled by data, but embrace fact-based changes
in business plans.

Top management of course still remains at the
helm of the enterprise. They chart the course, steer the
vessel, and thus define in what waters the enterprise
shall be making its way. Thereby they also define in
what areas of inquiry data scientists must focus their
attention. There is no substitute for this domain
expertise, this knowledge of where the biggest profit
opportunities (and often the most treacherous shoals
and currents) lie. Thus the value of the HiPPO
kingpins will morph from being seat-of-the-pants
dictators to simply knowing what questions to ask.

They'll be the proofs of Pablo Picasso's old admonition: "Computers are useless. They can only give you answers."

As in all things, leadership is critical when it comes to the practice of effective Data Science. Clear goals must be set. And they must be set by domain experts who understand how a market, discipline, or environment is developing, who can think in new ways and ponder novel solutions, who can embrace compelling new ideas – and can do all these things while at the same time balancing the needs of all stakeholders, including customers, stockholders, and employees.

Data Science demands practitioners with skill-sets not native to most enterprises – not even most IT departments. In particular we are talking about integrating statisticians (most of all statisticians skilled in the social sciences rather than business applications), programmers skilled in new non-traditional software such as Hadoop for cleaning and modeling unstructured data, and professionals skilled in predictive analysis and data visualization. These professionals – whose techniques along with their data are largely unstructured – occupy a previously undefined place on the map of the enterprise, one which lies in a one-time no-man's-land somewhere midway between the IT and marketing departments.

With these new professionals must come new chains of command, work-flow-practices, and procedures. Some toes will be stepped on. IT professionals and marketing professionals will lose some measure of autonomy. A new and expanded atmosphere of collaboration – both in practice and attitude – must be made to prevail. Most importantly, decision-making-rights must be adjusted and refined to reflect a shared collaborative environment which enables all to take ownership and act upon valid results, thus minimizing territoriality and what some consultants call the "not invented here" syndrome.

Let's face it. The introduction of a Data Science initiative to the enterprise is a tacit acknowledgment that existing methods of analytics, research, and innovation have fallen short. Any professionals associated with these legacy methods are going to feel upheaved and threatened. If management does not astutely handle the introduction of the new paradigm, giving all a sense of ownership, it is very easy for organizational infighting over data ownership, decision authority, and other issues to arise, costing time and money. On the other hand, when shared ownership and collaboration is made a top priority, the near-term result is far more likely to be a flowering of data-driven innovation, a rich Data Science culture, and clearly defined progress into new, previously unexplored and highly productive terrains of BI.

At the outset, the vision for a Data Science-driven model of decision making must be clearly enunciated and shared with all relevant staff, making them all stakeholders in the process. Once legacy professionals understand the prospects, and internalize the respect with which they are being consulted, they are far more likely to "buy-in" to the model and cooperate. (Note that the "buy-in" will prove essential. Although tasks can be commanded and responsibilities assigned, *enthusiasm* and *passion* cannot be. And these last two attributes are essential for success in Data Science, just as they are in most other things.)

Territoriality aside, most leading Data Science practitioners believe that the Data Science team should be located organizationally within whatever group "owns" the data, whether this be the IT department, the marketing/sales department, or some other division of the firm. Per Greenplum's Annika Jimenez, this centralized structure is important because "there is an essential collaboration which must exist between the data scientist and all the other owners of the 'value chain' of operationalized predictive and machine-learning models."

One last note on this topic: To build an effective Data Science team with the range of skills necessary, the enterprise will invariably need to budget for and hire new professionals to come on board, not to mention the acquisition of new data tools and technologies. At the same time however, it is critical to devise and implement training programs for any and all legacy staff whom the enterprise sees as becoming part of the new equation.

Avoiding Friction Between Old & New: Dealing with the TCQ Triangle

If you torture the data long enough, it will confess.
- Ronald Coase, Economist -

Managing a Data Science project tends to be quite a *fluid* process involving far more than just traditional planning and oversight. In these efforts, outcomes remain nebulous until they are reached; discovery of the unexpected is the order of the day; and set deadlines and benchmarks are not the norm. For traditionalists new to working with data scientists, the data scientists' methods can seem sloppy and disorganized – but it is important to realize that unique and often-foreign methods need to be adopted in order to isolate and interpret the granular data which the data scientist needs in order to achieve actionable BI.

The highly technical work of the "Quants" who are data scientists will often make their work seem obtuse and – indeed – eve sometimes even threatening to legacy employees. At the same time, the seemingly unorthodox methods of data scientists by their nature tend not to jive with the procedures and practices of other business units born of more traditional research and development models.

In the lion's share of organizations, line managers are the chief consumers of BI. But since many of these professionals tend not to be versed in Data Science procedures and methods, and are unable to evaluate the technical details of a project, they are often skeptical of results. Conversely, it is often the case that some data scientists – especially new hires and recent graduates – don't take enough into account the frontline business experience and seat-of-the-pants "know-how" that line managers often bring to the equation. Mutual respect and communication are essential, so that each camp can gain better insights by benefiting from the knowledge/expertise of the other.

The area of the most frequent disagreement is often what's called the *TCQ Triangle*.

TCQ stands for *Time*, *Cost*, and *Quality*.

Give less time while also limiting project costs, then end-result quality suffers. Give less time, but go with a less-restrictive budget, then you can get still a higher quality result. And – of course – if you want to do a project cheaply but still maintain the quality of your result, it is bound to take longer. Each angle of the triangle influences the other, inevitably.

When it comes to analytics projects, data scientists often find themselves at odds with others in the enterprise as regards to which is most important: time, money, or quality of results. Of course, it is an easy matter to measure time and cost – to benchmark these in the project plan. But it is a far harder thing to measure the impact of time and cost limitations on quality of results when it comes to granular Data Science research. Often, what seems like an "economical" project plan to the untutored eye, can be the most expensive of research scenarios in what it causes the Data Science analytics team to "miss." As one expert recently put it:

Risks to the organization grow when managers suspect that a data scientist's caveats about quality are simply "academic" concerns without long-term business consequences. ... Organizations ignore the costs of low quality in analytics projects at their peril. While data science within a business must be governed by prudent financial discipline, most experienced data scientists understand this. In many cases, though, the implication of lowering quality (to save money or time) is not an abstract or aesthetic issue. Rather, skimping on quality can have long-term implications. For example, it can make the difference between well-informed decisions and decisions that have key blind spots, or between strategies that are profitable and those that destroy value. It is often the case that a wrong answer is worse than no answer at all.

But there is nuance here; and once again we have a situation where dialogue between data scientists and line-managers/business-teams is vital. The nature of Data Science is that it tends to have few boundaries. Study and exploration can go on quite deeply – often more deeply than is necessary. It is important that data scientists have a firm grasp of in what explicit areas, what frontier, the line-managers and business-teams need good cartography, and where they don't. (*If the only interest is in the valley, don't bother exploring the mountain.*) Also, sometimes rough estimated results are just as useful as more refined information. It all depends on what questions are being asked.

In the end, it is important that the organization as a whole remains aware of what options are available, and the trade-offs the organization confronts in return for economies on time and budgets.

> *Against this backdrop, it is clear that a significant component of a data scientist's organizational role is to educate the organization about what is possible and, at the same time, to help other decision makers understand the consequences of reduced quality, shorter timelines, and smaller budgets that may result from different options. Because of their specialized backgrounds and expertise, data scientists are often uniquely positioned to inform these discussions within the organization.*

The Evolving Role
of the Data Scientist

The world is one big data problem.
- Andrew McAfee, *Center for Digital Business,*
MIT/Sloan -

Without Big Data, you are blind and deaf in the middle of a
freeway.
- Geoffrey Moore -

Data Science – once a new and novel niche in the enterprise – has now emerged as a driving force in the enterprise: a key component (if not *the* key component) of BI, overall strategic planning, and knowledge gathering.

Let's look at the timeline.

Data Science started out and had its infancy in the domain of academia, especially the social sciences. Academic researchers developed skills and algorithms for detecting economic, housing, and medical trends in specified populations. Their work was generally funded by grants. Their focus was on soft, non-commercial questions regarding quality of life and related issues, these questions addressed using traditional structured database models.

Following this, Data Science moved into corporate culture with the simple role of solving "point problems" – specifically-enunciated questions needing precise quantitative answers, these answers nearly always derived from one narrow, pre-defined source of *structured* data.

With the dawn of Big Data capabilities, Data Science emerged as a broadly defined endeavor breaking new ground, exploring the rapidly exploding and constantly flowing fonts of unstructured digital information in order to *generate new questions, define new pathways of BI, and become a force unto itself creatively driving and expanding the knowledge-base of the enterprise.*

And what of the future? Olly Downs, chief data scientist at the analytics firm Globys, says: "The way the Data Science role is migrating is that you don't just need to know your science and need to know about data – you need to now understand about technologies and the technology evolution to help you shape [strategy]. ... There are some big changes happening or about to come about … in how computation can be done and what sorts of algorithms are now scalable … . Problems that were exponentially hard to solve or algorithms that were exponentially hard to run but would really solve a problem correctly for you – a Data Science problem, or an optimization problem – it's going to become a reality that you can perform those computations. Now you need to understand how new types of computers work, in addition to understanding how new storage paradigms and data-representation paradigms work, and also still have at your core the understanding of statistics, machine learning, and data science."

Downs also sees the practice of Data Science spreading well beyond primary questions of markets, products, and customer service, and expanding dramatically to address more and more questions related to in-house efficiencies and cost-cutting. At such firms as General Motors, Data Science is already as much about safety, production practices, quality control, and human resources issues as it is about marketing, advertising, and customer demographics.

Another major area of new innovation will be the art and tools related to performing Data Science on information generated by the so-called "Internet of

Things" and wearable technologies. Here we are talking about tools and skills to help us manage and wrangle data related to ubiquitous location awareness along with location context. As Downs says: "It's more about the [location] sensing going everywhere with people and with physical things and [the proliferation of] that. It is about contextualizing that in time, which we're kind of used to, but also in physical or virtual space."

Throughout all of this, the definition of a data scientist – that rare Unicorn of the business world – will continue to be a creative "mash-up" of skills: hacker, analyst, programmer, statistician, communicator, market researcher, and – at times – clairvoyant.

In the final analysis few fields are as well positioned for exponential growth as is Data Science. The flood waters of Big Data will never stop rising – and with them both the promise and the problems of their enormity, velocity, and variety.

In other words, the promise and role of Data Science shall progress in step with the advance of technologies for generating, harvesting, and manipulating unstructured data. And these show every sign of conforming to the famous "Moore's

Law," originally promulgated decades ago by Gordon W. Moore, cofounder of Intel and Fairchild Semiconductor, which says, generally, that the speed and capabilities of data processing roughly double every two years. Thus far, Moore's Law has held up.

Ernest Dimnet has commented: "Too often we forget that genius, too, depends upon the data [knowledge] within its reach, that even Archimedes could not have devised Edison's inventions." Thus, as the capabilities and challenges of data technology advance, so will the evolving and increasingly vital role of the data scientist.

Data Science Ethics

and Privacy Concerns

You already have zero privacy – get over it.
- Scott McNealy, *Sun Microsystems* -

Few could miss the headlines about Facebook's infamous undisclosed January 2012 "mood experiment" on users. To recap, the study (published by researchers from Facebook, Cornell, and the University of California in the March 2013 *Proceedings of the National Academy of Sciences*) was designed to gage the social network's power to upset and/or excite people. The guinea pigs in the study were some 700,000 Facebook members who received News Feeds front-weighted with either positive or negative posts and images, this to see the extent to which their emotions could be impacted. Problem: The guinea pigs were never informed of their participation in the test.

In response to the uproar, Facebook COO Sheryl Sandberg explained: "This was part of ongoing research companies do to test different products, and that was what it was: it was poorly communicated. And for that communication we apologize. We never meant to upset you." It seems necessary to point out here that "poorly communicated" is Facebook lingo for "never communicated."

A subsequent Revolution Analytics survey of 144 data scientists attending the annual Joint Statistical Meetings of 2014 showed that a vast majority of data scientists and statisticians viewed the Facebook experiment as entirely unethical.

According to David Smith, chief community officer at Revolution Analytics, while data scientists and statisticians working in the health sciences field already have a great deal of regulation surrounding the way they collect and analyze data, tech and business industry standards and practices are "more opaque ... there's this whole new Wild West ... of data coming from Internet applications, Internet services, the Internet of Things, where these practices and procedures aren't really in place yet."

Clearly, Big Data creates numerous opportunities for misuse. Many data scientists see it as their job to create a rubric of ethical behavior in which their profession should place itself. One group which has taken on this job is a nonprofit founded in 2013 called the Data Science Association.

The code of ethics promulgated by this organization covers a range of areas, from protecting customer privacy to protecting practitioners from erroneous claims made by software innovators as to the efficacy of various Data Science tools.

For example, one item in the code insists that if a data scientist "reasonably believes a client is misusing Data Science to communicate a false reality or promote an illusion of understanding, the data scientist shall take reasonable remedial measures, including disclosure to the client, and including, if necessary, disclosure to the proper authorities. The data scientist shall take reasonable measures to persuade the client to use Data Science appropriately."

As the widely critical reaction to the Facebook study suggests, one of the chief ethical dilemmas confronting the data scientist is balancing transparency and a basic respect for privacy with the need to legitimately accumulate and use data for research purposes.

On the up-side, most users of the Internet rather enjoy having Amazon of Netflix suggest books, music, and films based on their prior purchases and clear preferences. Most also enjoy when Facebook makes solid recommendations for likely new friends, and when LinkedIn proposes a business connection which makes sense. But all of these conveniences – all of these results of Data Science – come at a cost. And that cost is the sacrifice of some measure of privacy.

Research shows that at the same time as users enjoy the perks enumerated above, they also resent the loss of privacy. A recent Pew Research *Internet and American Life* study shows that 86 percent of Internet users have taken at least some steps towards removing or masking their identities while online. Some data gathering firms, attempting to address this, have been quite pro-active and open concerning their business models. Acxiom Corporation, for example, is a firm solely focused on the acquisition and sale of data on individuals and corporations. They've recently launched aboutthedata.com, a site where users can see and control what Acxiom knows about them and their online habits.

Overall, however, the ethics concerning the gathering, use, and analysis of customer information remains very fuzzy, to say the least. "Generally speaking," says Dr. Rachel Schutt of Columbia University's Institute for Data Sciences and

Engineering, "fields such as statistics, computer science and the hard sciences don't teach ethics. [Sure] there are privacy concerns ... but software engineers [are only taught] about the elegance or the mathematical beauty of the thing they're building, not how it will affect people's lives."

Karrie Karahalios, Computer Science Professor at the Univeristy of Illinois Champaign-Urbana points out that "If you do these large social network studies, you don't have what they call participant-informed consent. Let's say I have you in one of my Facebook studies, and you're coming to my lab and we are analyzing the strength of the connections between you and your friends. I'm getting information about your friends and their friends without their consent. It's a very, very ethically sensitive area."

In academic settings there have long been some protections in effect via guidelines promulgated in 1978's Belmont Report – guidelines designed to protect the identities and interests of human research subjects. But these guidelines – adherence to which are a prerequisite to any Federal funding – chiefly address subjects engaged in *voluntary direct research after having given informed consent to the research being transacted.* "This is where it gets interesting with Big Data, because there are a lot of things you can do with

Big Data that don't involve talking with people," says Karahalios. "If your study involves just scraping the Web, and not talking to a human, you don't have to [worry about the Belmont Report]."

When it comes to non-academic studies such as those conducted by Data Science teams within commercial enterprises, such items as the Belmont Report don't even apply. Users are particularly exposed and at risk when they participate in open social networks such as Facebook or Instagram, or maintain a Google identity (including gmail) or use a free e-mail service such as Yahoo. The general policy of such organizations is that the user "pays" for participation on their service(s) by sacrificing some measure of privacy. The currency paid is personal data – buying habits, etc.

Confusion shall prevail for the forseeable future.

"There are academic workshops on the governance of algorithms," says Dr. Schutt, "and I know that high-level executives from major corporations go to Washington and have meetings, but I don't think there's a uniform policy or standardization for what should be done with user-level data. We've been looking to companies like Google or Facebook to do the right thing and to set the standard but to the extent these are enforced or that other companies have to follow, a lot of this stuff isn't in place … It's the sort of thing where … [many] people don't object and it doesn't seem that bad, but it really opens the door up to worse things."

Indeed it does.

The Art of

Seeing Things

There is a magic in graphs. The profile of a curve reveals in a flash a whole situation – the life history of an epidemic, a panic, or an era of prosperity. The curve informs the mind, awakens the imagination, convinces.
- Henry D. Hubbard, 1939 -

Much of our best analytical thinking is graphically-oriented. By conceptualizing and rendering data in a visual manner, we make it easier for ourselves to detect, study, and understand patterns within that data, thus enabling greater insight and facilitating greater creative thinking about the data. Human perception and cognition thrive and are enhanced in such an environment.

In the conduct of data visualization, data scientists use everything from the most simple charts and graphs (such as have been found in scientific texts going back for centuries) to two-dimensional vector graphics and even some images enhanced with animation and viewer-interactivity. The data scientist also uses hierarchical layouts and networks (for visualizing relationships) and – most importantly – tools for the visualization of databases and data mining processes, especially the visualization of such unstructured data as are the data scientist's stock and trade.

Noted information designer David McCandless tells us that "by visualizing information, we turn it into a landscape that you can explore with your eyes, a sort of information map. And when you're lost in information, an information map is kind of useful." OK, so data visualization creates a map. Good. More formally, data visualization can be described as: "the abstraction of information in schematic form, including attributes or variables for the units of information."

Visualizations are especially valuable when it comes to extremely large data sets such as data scientists confront daily. Even with enormous data volumes, the right graphic rendering, or collection of graphic renderings, can help people spot patterns more easily and quickly than via any other method – grasping facts which would not otherwise be obvious.

But it is very easy to over-reach when doing graphic visualizations of data – to unwittingly go for art instead of information. This should, of course, be guarded against.

According to Dr. Jerome Friedman, professor of Statistics at Stamford, the "main goal of data visualization is to communicate information clearly and effectively through graphical means. It doesn't mean that data visualization needs to look boring to be functional or extremely sophisticated to look beautiful. To convey ideas effectively, both aesthetic form and functionality need to go hand in hand, providing insights into a rather sparse and complex data set by communicating its key-aspects in a more intuitive way. Yet designers often fail to achieve a balance between form and function, creating gorgeous data visualizations which fail to serve their main purpose – to communicate information."

We've all heard the phrase "simple is better." We've all encountered the famous quote from Henry David Thoreau: "Simplify, simplify." A large part of the job of a well-constructed visualization is to remove as much unnecessary complexity as possible while still remaining true, accurate, and useful. Thus, whatever the form of the visualization – be it a simple chart or an elegant, integrated animation – it should be streamlined to embrace only the most essential variables and exclude any and all extraneous data. By this we do not mean excluding data that does not tend toward a particular pre-defined result. Hardly. But we *do* mean to exclude data which is *irrelevant* to ascertaining an accurate result.

With an increasing number of "gee-whiz" simple, powerful (and, frankly, *fun*) data visualization tools at our fingertips everyday, there is always a great temptation to "over-design" our graphics, thus eliminating the very simplicity which is their goal, and thus also making it harder – not easier – to spot patterns. As one data visualization guru has explained: "The best design gets out of the way between the viewer's brain and the content."

Noah Illinsky, an IBM visualization expert, tells us that "despite what you were told in school, most people don't care about seeing your work. They don't care about how much data you can process every day or how big your Hadoop cluster is. Customers and internal users want specific, relevant answers, and the sooner they can get those answers, the better. The closer you can come to giving them exactly what they want, the less effort they have to expend looking for answers. Any irrelevant data on the page makes finding the relevant information more difficult; irrelevant data (no matter how valid) is noise."

And noise is what we want to avoid at all costs.

In explaining his thesis that "most people's charts and graphics look like crap," commentator Ross Crooks makes the seemingly-obvious but often ignored point that "good data visualization relies on good design. And it's about more than just choosing the right chart type. It's about presenting information in a way that is easy to understand and intuitive to navigate, making the viewer do as little legwork as possible. Of course, not all designers are data visualization experts, which is why much of the visual content we see is, well, less than stellar."

The fundamental rules are so full of common sense they barely need to be enunciated:

Don't use complex animations when a simple pie-chart will do the trick. Don't arrange data non-intutively. Don't design in a way which obscures relevant data. *Never* use 3-D animations, which distort perception and thus can skew the viewer's understanding of data. Assure data is presented and understood accurately by sticking to 2-D shapes. Finally, *never* go for what "looks good" over what is clean, precise, accurate, and easily-digested.

Writing in his now-classic book *The Visual Display of Quantitative Information*, Edward Tufte tells us: "Graphical excellence is that which gives to the viewer the greatest number of ideas in the shortest time with the least ink in the smallest space." To this he adds a salient warning. "Cosmetic decoration, which frequently distorts the data, will never salvage an underlying lack of content."

In sum, the role of data visualization in Data Science is two-fold.

Early in the process, well-designed visualizations help the data scientist discern and discover new trends and patterns in data which in turn yield hints for further research and/or indicate actionable BI results. With this tool the data scientist makes initial discoveries. The data scientist and his team are the consumers and users of the visualizations at this stage of the process.

At the conclusion of the process, visualizations must be created, customized, and geared toward explaining results to the ultimate consumers of the research – people beyond the Data Science team. This is where concise simplicity is most needed: telling the story of the research and results cogently and efficiently, with a minimum of that odious thing called *noise*.

Data

Management

The function of good software is to make the complex appear to be simple.

- Grady Booch -

The right data management tools are key to making effective use of Big Data, turning its volume into a resource rather than a daunting mountain of unsorted bits and bytes. With the right data management techniques tools, Big Data can be divided relatively easily into manageable chunks.

Data analytics empower firms to dissect and study sets of data that matter most to them and their business goals.

Data capture is what's going on when firms get people to sign up to various things, asking for details at all opportunities and collecting consumer insight based on the accumulated data. However, none of it will make much sense unless the useful data sets have been directly identified.

Data management constitutes the systematic approach to dicing and slicing massive piles of data into logical, digestible portions.

The key step to effective data management is defining and adopting a comprehensive, systematic process for using Big Data. A major component of this is to centralize all information collected into a single place, rather than using disparate systems. Data quality software integration, together with data visualization tools, can help achieve this primary step: putting data into the right context, and in this way making it meaningful.

Once this is achieved, it becomes far easier to get the right data into the right hands. XMG analyst Jacky Garrido has commented in a *ZDnet* interview that enterprises must isolate the right sorts of data in order "to avoid getting buried under the humongous amount of information they generate through various outlets." Garrido compares Big Data to an ocean wave; companies must either ride on top of or be consumed by it."

Analytics for Big Data can involve any number of procedures, some deriving from the pure traditional sciences of uinivariate, bivariate, and multivariate analysis. Of course, univariate analysis refers to the study of single-variables, bivariate to the study of two, and multivariate to the application of univariate and bivariate procedures, plus other procedures, to multiple variables.

Stream Processing (aka, Real Time Analytic Processing – RTAP)

Remember how we said one key characteristic of Big Data is *velocity*? Yes, well that being the case, the data scientist is not so much interested in looking at a traditional "data set" as he or she is in studying "data streams." The data scientist must mine and analyze actionable data in real time using architectures that are capable of processing streams of data *as they occur*. This is a major area of Big Data and Data Science where the best and most robust tools are still in the making. All in all, current database paradigms are not ideal for stream processing, although the algorithms already exist.

As Mike Driscoll notes: " … Calculating an average over a group of data can be done in a traditional batch process, but far more efficient algorithms exist for calculating a moving average of data as it arrives, incrementally, unit by unit. If you want to take a repository of data and perform almost any statistical analysis, that can be accomplished with open source products like R or commercial products like SAS. But if you want to create a set of streaming statistics, to which you incrementally add or remove a chunk of data as a moving average, the libraries either don't exist or are immature."

Artificial Intelligence,

Machine Learning,

and Deep Learning

in Data Science

You can use all the quantitative data you can get, but you still have to distrust it and use your own intelligence and judgment.
- Alvin Toffler -

The question of whether a computer can think is no more interesting than the question of whether a submarine can swim.
- Edsger W. Dijkstra -

Computers will never replace the intuitive role of the human element vis-a-vis Data Science research. Let me repeat that. Computers will *never* replace the intuitive role of the human element vis-a-vis Data Science research.

What current and developing Artificial Intelligence (AI) software *can* and will do, however, is *help facilitate* the parsing of various dark data, especially dark data which needs to be gathered from such esoteric sources as images and digital recordings of telephone conversations with customers.

AI applications are very good at recognizing and responding to inputs. Ask an AI app linked to an extensive database to give the name of the man who was President during the American Depression, and it will tell you "Franklin Delano Roosevelt." Posit the speculative question as to whether the Rooseveltian "New Deal" programs sped up or (as some people argue) slowed down the recovery, and the AI application will come up with … *nothing*.

Speculation, imagination, and conjecture are not attributes which lie within the realm of machines. (A note here. Even fact-based questions can be flubbed by AI apps, depending on the quality and nuance and detail of the data originally input. In training to go on the game show *Jeopardy*, IBM's "Watson" answered "Wonder Woman" when asked to name the first female to go into space. The data input never separated fictional women from nonfictional women. And the machine was only as good as its data.)

What an AI application – in this example, a natural language processing AI system – *can* do, however, is take digital recordings of inbound customer-service phone calls and identify all instances of the words "complaint," "dissatisfied," and "unhappy," then match these instances with the words "delivery," "installation," and "hot-tub," to derive data as to what aspects of your hot-tub sales business have annoyed those customers who have wound up annoyed. Data scientists can then pair this data with other references, such as geographical region, time of year, hot-tub model, and so forth to derive actionable BI. *What the computer cannot do is deliver a qualitative analysis based on these quantitative results.* For that we need humans.

The machine is, however, capable of dealing with rudimentary *fact-based what-if* scenarios – scenarios which must first be imagined and conjectured by human data scientists posing the right questions upon the right data.

For example, factoring in prescribed mean average temperatures throughout the year as segmented by geographical region, and the minimum temperature necessary for the putty involved with hot-tub installation to settle correctly, and pairing this data with customer complaints related to "installation" segmented by region, *where are the dateline "tipping-points" at which installations can best proceed and had best stop in Maine as opposed to Ohio?* This type of thing the machine can handle. But the intuition to pose the question remains, and always will remain, within the human sphere.

In short, AI applications for Data Science – of which there are more and more being released every day – are perfectly capable of combining multiple data points and isolating patterns in data; but it is up to the data scientist to postulate which patterns to look for, and to draw and/or infer conclusions from those patterns. So-called "machine learning" apps with "intelligent-seeming algorithms" can certainly handle sophisticated statistical analysis. Indeed, they can even get better at this over time, on their own; but they will never be capable of creative curiosity and intuitiveness.

Yann LeCun, director of Artificial Intelligence at Facebook, stresses how very important it is to understand the line between human thinking and AI Machine Learning, most especially the latest focus of Machine Learning called "Deep Learning" with neural networks.

LeCun doesn't like it when people say "[Deep Learning] works just like a brain." As LeCun explains, although "Deep Learning gets [its] inspiration from biology, it's very, very far from what the brain actually does. And describing it like the brain gives a bit of the aura of magic to it, which is dangerous. It leads to hype; people claiming things that are not true."

In clearly defining the separation of the human and computing aspects of Data Science, LeCun captures the essence and the poetry of this interaction, and how one aspect enhances the value of the other. "It's very much an interplay between intuitive insights, theoretical modeling, practical implementations, empirical studies, and scientific analyses," says LeCun. "The insight is creative thinking, the modeling is mathematics, the implementation is engineering and sheer hacking, the empirical study and the analysis are actual science. What I am most fond of are beautiful and simple theoretical ideas that can be translated into something that works."

Still, the value of Deep Learning as applied to Data Science, even though over-hyped, should nonetheless not be underestimated. Gary Marcus, cognitive professor at NYU explains the technology in the most succinct and understandable manner. He writes that: "A computer is confronted with a large set of data, and on its own asked to sort the elements of that data into categories, a bit like a child who is asked to sort a set of toys, with no specific instructions. The child might sort them by color, by shape, or by function, or by something else. Machine learners try to do this on a grander scale, seeing, for example, millions of handwritten digits, and making guesses about which digits looks more like one another, 'clustering' them together based on similarity. Deep Learning's important innovation is to have models learn categories incrementally, attempting to nail down lower-level categories (like letters) before attempting to acquire higher-level categories (like words)."

This subtle interaction of Deep Learning technologies and human intuition is what Eric Berridge, CEO of Bluewolf, alludes to when he says: "Perfect Data Science takes every customer interaction and identifies patterns that can be repeated and proactively acted upon. In this ideal scenario, humans and artificial intelligence systems collaborate in an amalgamation of contextual, timely insight to better understand their customers and, ultimately, to predict their future behaviors."

Data Curation

And

The Tribal Knowledge

Problem

Data, I think, is one of the most powerful mechanisms for telling stories. I take a huge pile of data and I try to get it to tell stories.
- Steven Levitt, economist -

Not everything that can be counted counts, and not everything that counts can be counted.
- Albert Einstein -

The phrase Big Data encompasses both the opportunity and the problem confronting data scientists. That the data is so vast means great, *never-before-possible* opportunities for harvesting actionable BI. The problem, meanwhile, remains the very vastness of this sea of data, and exactly how to structure and curate this enormous chaos of unstructured data in a way which yields *the most valuable* actionable BI.

F. Scott Fitzgerald said of his novels that it took only a few seconds to conceive them, months to write [curate] them, and his "entire life" to create the memories and experiences which comprised his own vast sea of unstructured data – combining disparate emotions, memories, and wisdom to create a new, vibrant revelation in story form.

Andy Palmer, co-founder of the firms Vertica Systems and Tamir, insists Data Science is "really not about Big Data. It's about the most *useful* data." Vertica and Tamir, along with many other companies, focus on delivering to enterprises various technologies with which they can quickly discover the so-called "dark data" that's most relevant, and often hidden, but of a quality which can answer what Palmer calls "compelling questions." This task is called *data curation* – also sometimes referred to in the industry as *data wrangling, plumbing, "munging,"* and *janitor work.*

Firms such as Vertica Systems, Tamir, and other startups develop and offer a range of software tools aimed at helping data scientists curate unstructured data economically and productively. Some firms focus on software designed to "synchronize" data feeding in from disparate, otherwise unrelated business systems within the enterprise – such as customer relationship management (aka, CRM) data, marketing data, e-mail data, and finance data. Other firms develop and offer data-prep tools designed to automate the otherwise laborious "extract, transform, and load" (aka, ETL) chore involved in cleaning data for storage in data warehouses.

On the analytics end of the equation, firms such as Cloudera, Hadapt, and Hortonworks create and distribute software designed to enhance the open-source analytics platform Hadoop and make it even more robust than it is in its native state. Add to this even more firms developing and distributing tools for exploration of vertical and niche data which leverage R and Python, the leading open-source languages used by data scientists. (I'll discuss a bit more about Hadoop and R in the next chapter.)

Boston's Doug Levin, the founder of Black Duck Software and CEO of Quant5, sums things up vis-a-vis data curation and the tools associated with that curation when he tells us "enabling data-driven decisions in corporations is one of today's most significant technology trends." Levin further reminds us that the ability of data scientists to manipulate, organize, and study unstructured data is quickly advancing past the previous limits of Big Data analytics into vital new frontiers.

Data curation is the solution to what some call the "Tribal Knowledge Problem."

What is The Tribal Knowledge Problem?

If you've ever had a business question to which you needed an answer and were referred by someone in the finance department to "go ask Brad in Personnel," then you've experienced The Tribal Knowledge Problem. Although the solution to the problem in this simple scenario is as easy as taking a stroll and questioning Brad, that solution does not scale in the digital space where lurks Big Data. The quest is for the right data hidden behind disparate data sources. Curation must bring order to the chaos and fight darkness with light, defining the truly relevant data as narrowly as possible. In short, in the digital space, we need sophisticated software tools and approaches to get us to Brad and solicit his answer.

The traditional master data management (aka, MDM) top-down approach of carefully-defined categorization is useless in this scenario because of the great velocity with which data sources and data types change within the Big Data environment.

"While everybody is focused on the problem of how to visualize the data and how to make the compute go faster and how to store the information more efficiently," says Alation's Satyen Sangani, "we've seen little about the fact that there's just so much more data out there [and therefore] a fundamental information relevance problem. How do you get the [right] data when you need it. How do you sort through it? How do you filter down the data to get what you're actually looking for?" That's the fundamental problem.

"The problem with MDM is it's effectively all top down human curation," comments Sangani. "Our observation has been that's just not scalable. It never was scalable previously … but it works even less now. If you think about the amount of data that's being generated, that's one factor. But the data is also becoming more complicated. On top of that, there's just very little in resources to manage the data. There has to be more people managing the data, more people accessing and touching the data, to talk about it and describe it. But there also have to be automated techniques in order to enable the people who do that management work faster."

"Big Data's fine," writes Gigaom's Barb Darrow. "The *right* data, however, is a game changer." Here we are talking about refining, getting to, and leveraging that precise vertical data set – that *niche* data set – which is Brad. That's the challenge. And that's the mission of data curation. Without the skills and tools to "go narrow" in our focus and pick just the right information stream or information streams from the vast and continually flowing data rivers, the entire ecosystem is useless for BI purposes. Thus arises that most vital task called data curation.

Data
Cleaning

There are three kinds of lies: lies, damned lies, and statistics.

- George Bernard Shaw -

Data cleaning (sometimes also referred to as data cleansing or data scrubbing) is the act of detecting and either removing or correcting corrupt or inaccurate records from a record set, table, or database. Used mainly in cleansing databases, the process applies identifying incomplete, incorrect, inaccurate, irrelevant, etc. items of data and then replacing, modifying, or deleting this "dirty" information.

The next step after data cleaning is *data reduction*. This includes defining and extracting attributes, decreasing the dimensions of data, representing the problems to be solved, summarizing the data, and selecting portions of the data for analysis.

Generally, in order to be classified as "high-quality," data needs to pass a firm and exacting set of criteria. Those include:

Accuracy: an aggregated value over the criteria of integrity, consistency, and density

Integrity: an aggregated value over the criteria of completeness and validity

Completeness: achieved by correcting data containing anomalies

Validity: approximated by the amount of data satisfying integrity constraints

Consistency: concerns contradictions and syntactical anomalies

Uniformity: directly related to irregularities and in compliance with the set "unit of measure"

Density: the quotient of missing values in the data and the number of total values ought to be known

Sharon Machlis of *ComputerWorld* puts data cleaning into perspective: "Before you can analyze and visualize data, it often needs to be 'cleaned.' What does that mean? Perhaps some entries list 'New York City' while others say 'New York, NY' and you need to standardize them before you can see patterns. There might be some records with misspellings or numerical data-entry errors." Such procedures as this constitute data cleaning.

Note: The need to analyze time-series or other forms of streaming (velocity) data poses unique data cleaning challenges. Examples of this class of data include economic time-series like stock prices, exchange rates, or unemployment figures, biomedical data sequences like electrocardiograms or electroencephalograms, or industrial process operating data sequences like temperatures, pressures or concentrations. Nevertheless fundamental principles of data cleaning apply just as much to these data sets as to any others.

Bruce Ratner, Ph.D. – of the highly-regarded *DM Stat-1 Consulting* – identifies ten fundamentals of data cleaning:

1. Check frequencies of continuous and categorical variables for unreasonable distributions.

2. Check frequencies of continuous and categorical variables for detection of unexpected values. For continuous variables, look into data "clumps" and "gaps."

3. Check for improbable values (e.g., a boy named Sue), and impossible values (e.g., age is 120 years young, and x/0).

4. Check the type for numeric variables: Decimal, integer, and date.

5. Check the meanings of misinformative values, e.g., "NA", the blank " ", the number "0", the letter "O", the dash "-", and the dot ". ".

6. Check for out-of-range data: Values "far out" from the "fences" of the data.

7. Check for outliers: Values "outside" the fences of the data.

8. Check for missing values, and the meanings of their coded values, e.g., the varied string of "9s", the number "0", the letter "O", the dash "-", and the dot ". ".

9. Check the logic of data, e.g., response rates cannot be 110%, and weigh contradictory values, along with conflict resolution rules, e.g., duplicate records of BR's DOB: 12/22/56 and 12/22/65.

10. Last but not least, check for the typos.

Ratner: "After the ten basic and analyst-specific checks are done, data cleaning is not completed until the *noise* in the data is eliminated. Noise is the idiosyncrasies of the data: The particulars, the "nooks and crannies" that are not part of the sought-after essence (e.g., predominant pattern) of the data with regard to the objective of the analysis/model. Ergo, the data particulars are lonely, not-really-belonging-to pieces of information that happen to be both in the population from which the data was drawn and in the data itself (what an example of a double-chance occurrence!) Paradoxically, as the analyst includes more and more of the prickly particulars in the analysis/model, the analysis/model becomes better and better, yet the analysis/model validation becomes worse and worse. Noise must be eliminated from the data."

Data Modeling

For

Unstructured Data

It is a capital mistake to theorize before one has data.

\- Sherlock Holmes -

Data modeling is the analysis of data objects used in a business or other context and the identification of the relationships among these data objects. Another definition, this from Scott Ambler, Chief Methodologist for Agile and Lean within IBM Rational: "Data modeling is the act of exploring data-oriented structures. Like other modeling artifacts data models can be used for a variety of purposes, from high-level conceptual models to physical data models."

The sheer quantity and complexity of unstructured data opens up many new opportunities for the analyst and modeler. Imagine requirements such as: Show me consumer feedback on my product from all Website discussion groups for the last six months; Show me all photographs taken of the fountains in Rome from the summers of 2002 through 2007; Show me all contracts which contain a particular liability clause.

"So – what is a data model?" asks David Dichmann, Product Line Director for Design Tools at Sybase. "It is first and foremost a way to capture business language and information relationships that provide context to make it useful in decision making activities. It is then specialized into representations of storage paradigms, and ultimately, when appropriate, into detailed designs of physical systems where structures will be implemented to manage, store, move, transform and analyze data points. Today's data models are way beyond traditional logical/physical representations of database systems implementation. Today's data models are architectural drawings of the meaning and intent of information – simple, beautiful creations that drive the logic of applications, systems and technology and physical implementations of business information infrastructure."

Dichmann posits that the data model, if viewed as "an abstraction of the physical representation of the database structures," clearly declines in value in face of the schema-less [data] or the constantly changing schemas. "But, if it is the abstraction of the conceptual representation of the information, we see a rise in importance. The language of the business, and the context of data points, provide meaning to the analysis that we want to gain from these non-traditional systems. [We are on a journey] from points of data (records collected by recording all our 'transactions') to meaningful information (the collation, aggregation and analysis of points of data by applying context to data). With Big Data, we do not even consider the data points themselves but rather jump right to some trend analysis (aggregation of sorts). Interpretation comes from comparisons to a series of basis points to be used in decision making, taking data all the way to wisdom. The basis points themselves are context and can be modeled."

Some posit that with regard to big data, data modeling is a major obstacle to agile business intelligence (BI). The answer, according leading software analyst Barney Finucane.

"The need for data modeling depends upon the application. [Software] products that promise user friendly analysis without any data analysis are usually intended for a specific type of analysis that does not require any previously specified structure." A good example of data that does not require modeling is what retailers gather about their customers. "This data comes in big flat tables with many columns, and the whole point to the analysis is to find unexpected patterns in this unstructured data. In this case adding a model is adding assumptions that may actually hinder the analysis process."

However, "some types of analyses only make sense with at least some modeling. Time intelligence is an example of a type of analysis that is supported by a data model. Also analyzing predefined internal structures such as cost accounts or complex sales channels is usually more convenient based on predefined structures. The alternative method of discovering the structures in the raw data may not be possible."

Finucane adds: "Planning is a common area of agile BI, and planning is rarely possible without predefined structures. It is no coincidence that the tools that promise analysis without data modeling do not offer planning features. Planning requires adding new data to an existing data set. In some cases, this includes adding new master data, for example when new products are being planned. Furthermore, there is often a good deal of custom business logic in a planning application that cannot be defined automatically. Most financial planning processes, and the analysis and simulation that goes along with them cannot be carried out on a simple table. In my view the new generation columnar databases are a welcome addition to agile BI. But I also think that their marketing is sometimes a little over the top when it comes to dismissing existing BI solution in this area."

Forrester Research analyst James Kobielus goes a step further: "Big data relies on solid data modeling. Statistical predictive models and test analytic models will be the core applications you will need to do big data."

But Brett Sheppard, executive director at Zettaforce and a former senior analyst at Gartner, disagrees. "Letting data speak for itself through analysis of entire data sets is eclipsing modeling from subsets. In the past, all too often what were once disregarded as 'outliers' on the far edges of a data model turned out to be the telltale signs of a micro-trend that became a major event. To enable this advanced analytics and integrate in real-time with operational processes, companies and public sector organizations are evolving their enterprise architectures to incorporate new tools and approaches."

Ultimately, it is important to remember re: data modeling for Big Data is that any given model is just a simplified representation of reality and can take many forms.

One of the best tools for the modeling of unstructured data is Apache Cassandra, this to be discussed at length in a subsequent chapter. The most important aspect of Cassandra and other such tools is that they allow the flexibility required to ensure data models are scaled in a way that is cost-effective with regard to unstructured Big Data, especially the application of multidimensional data models, vertical industry data models and customizable analytics problem algorithms.

In the final analysis, a data model for Big Data is useless without the human element: the skilled eye of the data scientist, discerning subtleties ('outliers') in data. "Data sparsity, non-linear interactions and the resultant model's quirks must be interpreted through the lens of domain expertise," writes Ben Gimpert of Altos Research. "All Big Data models are wrong but some are useful, to paraphrase the statistician George Box. A data scientist working in isolation could train a predictive model with perfect in-sample accuracy, but only an understanding of how the business will use the model lets [him or her] balance the crucial bias/variance trade-off. *Put more simply, applied business knowledge is how we can assume a model trained on historical data will do decently with situations we have never seen."*

Predictive
Analysis

It is tough to make predictions, especially about the future.

- Yogi Berra -

Tech journalist Jon Gertner has written: "It now seems possible that the [social] networks' millions of posts and status updates are adding up to something culturally and financially priceless." In a recent piece for *The New York Times*, Gertner cited to key examples:

1. HP Labs has developed an algorithm that analyzes Twitter messages about newly released films. The results are used to predict how well these films will perform at the box office long-term, and the algorithm has thus far out-performed (in terms of accuracy) a long-standing tool called the Hollywood Stock Exchange used for the same purpose.

2. A research team at Indiana University recently classified close to 10 million tweets into six "mood categories" (alertness, calmness, happiness, kindness, sureness, and vitality). The team leader, Johan Bollen, was actually surprised to find that the results "could predict changes in the Dow Jones Industrial Average." Bollen says he expected the mood on Twitter would be a *reflection* of up and down movements in the stock market. He never imagined it would be a precursor. But it is.

As Gertner writes: "Social scientists have begun looking more broadly at the aggregate value of social media." Thus the rise of predictive analysis as the key to extracting maximum business intelligence from this Big Data.

Predictive analysis gives organizations full investigative power to delve into any corner of data to discover otherwise obscure details behind specific performance outcomes. The main idea of predictive analysis is to use current and past data to predict future events. The goal of the statistical techniques used in predictive analysis is to determine market patterns, identify risks, and predict potential opportunities for growth. In addition, data relationships can be reordered to determine the most plausible outcome of possible solutions and patterns can be recognized that might have the power to alter the outcome of a probable event.

Eric Robson, leader of the Data Mining and Social Networks Analysis Group at the TSSG, a part of Ireland's Waterford Institute of Technology, explains: "For instance, a large supermarket has many thousands of customers and many thousands of products to sell. Usually each customer is tracked via their charge card ... and we are able to see return visits. On day one, a customer might buy bread and some butter. On day three, they buy some more bread but it might not be until day fourteen that they need to buy some more butter. From this simple example we can see how a trend or a purchasing pattern can be determined." *This*, then, is predictive analysis.

Robson continues: "In social network predictive analytics people are constantly passing messages to each other. From a marketing perspective we can look at who we should be targeting to send our viral message out to for further [propagation.] Who are the biggest distributors of content? It may not necessarily be commercial entities. It could be; bloggers, people with very active Facebook accounts, people with very active Twitter accounts. In terms of product, we can start identifying who are the key influencers. Say, IOracle Advanced Analytics Option wanted to sell something like running shoes and this guy is a marathon runner and blogs about them. If we know that people listen to him then the running shoe manufacturer can start targeting this guy. 'Here's a free pair of running shoes. Tell us what you think of them.' More importantly, 'Tell the world what you think of them.'"

In the past, marketers would use relatively small numbers to extrapolate a larger result. With social media, they can look at thousands or millions of opinions and come to conclusions that lead to refreshing existing campaigns or creating new ones. They can analyze raw consumer opinion at its source – this more likely to reveal the unvarnished truth, unlike the sometimes false positives often derived via focus groups and surveys.

Numerous firms offer superior software applications which make predictive analysis a relatively easy task – at least from a technical viewpoint.

A Bit More on Data Visualization (*or* Telling the Story)

A picture is worth a thousand words.

"If you're trying to extract useful information from an ever-increasing inflow of data, you'll likely find *visualization* useful – whether it's to show patterns or trends with graphics instead of mountains of text, or to try to explain complex issues to a nontechnical audience." So writes *InfoWorld's* Sharon Machlis.

Rebeckah Blewett, product manager for Dundas Data Visualization Inc., explains: "The practice of representing information visually is nothing new. Scientists, students, and analysts have been using data visualization for centuries to track everything from astrological phenomena to stock prices." Data visualization, when done correctly, is a highly effective way to analyze large amounts of data to identify correlations, trends, outliers, patterns, and business conditions.

Many of us have experienced rudimentary forms of data visualization in our day-to-day experience of the Web. The popular TwitterEarth, for example, shows real-time tweets from all over the world on a 3D globe. It's a great visualization tool to see where tweets are coming from in real time and discover new people to follow. It's also fascinating just to sit and watch. Another simple example is the Flickr Related Tag Browser, which allows you to search for a series of tags and see related tags. Clicking on a different tag brings up new related tags. You can zoom into the tag selected in the center of the screen by hovering and see images tagged with that word. It also gives a total image count and lets you browse by page. And another is TED Sphere, which shows videos from the TED conference in a spherical format with 3D navigation. You can view the sphere from inside or outside and the layout of videos is based on semantic compatibility.

Data presentation can be beautiful, elegant and descriptive," writes Vitaly Freidman of *Smashing Magazine*. "There is a variety of conventional ways to visualize data -tables, histograms, pie charts and bar graphs are being used every day, in every project and on every possible occasion. However, to convey a message ... effectively, sometimes you need more than just a simple pie chart of your results. In fact, there are much better, profound, creative and absolutely fascinating ways to visualize data. Many of them might become ubiquitous in the next few years."

In essence, the task of data visualization involves creating data layers and presenting these as easy-to-comprehend graphics for viewing by data analysts and non-tech decision-makers. Think of it as the graphical blending of data.

"Graph-based visual analysis is a highly effective method for capturing and understanding relationships between data that are not quantitative in nature," writes industry pundit Jin H. Kim. "This method and technology has been used in diverse fields such as intelligence and law enforcement to customer sentiment and network topology analysis to uncover hidden insights in growing data that was not possible when relying only on traditional analytics."

Kim continues: "The combination of rich data collection, advanced analytics operating across both structured and unstructured data, and efficiently storing and analyzing information in quantities unimagined just a few years back, have created a new era of data analysis in general and visual analysis in particular. We can now look at the networks representing relationships between data as not just static topologies, but rather as 'dynamic networks' with their own behavioral pattern in terms of change, sequence of change, and uncertainties of change, combined with the ability to integrate information from complex event processing engines and other 'event driven' information sources. These new developments promise to bring about a new dawn of information use, enabling smarter, timelier decision-making in various fields of human endeavor."

As suggested previously (ala Twitter), data visualization plays a key role in real-time structured network analysis (SNA) – the modeling of relationships and overlaps between disparate groups of people.

"Social network analysis uses graph theoretic ideas and applies them with the premise that the structure of the graph can be used to understand and identify critical relationships and influential people. ... " writes Elizabeth Hefner of Tom Sawyer Software. " Recent advancements in network analysis involving complex network topologies with multiple relationships between nodes, network behavior that is based on uncertain information, and time-based change of networks, have enhanced the value of incorporating advanced network analysis techniques as a key part of an analytics tool-set to aid in better understanding data relationships. More organizations are beginning to understand that with advanced visual analysis technology, they can build integrated insights across all of their available data, enabling them to better understand emerging opportunities and threats. ... The combination of advanced visualization techniques, together with social network analysis techniques, will help bridge the emerging gap between the vast amounts of available information in Big Data and the available resources to better understand them."

Numerous firms provide quite elegant, effective and powerful tools for data visualization.

These are just two options among many.

Edward Tufte – author of the classic *Visual Display of Quantitative Information* – has written: "The commonality between science and art is in trying to see profoundly – to develop strategies of seeing and showing." No truer words.

Cassandra

There's a way to do it better – find it.

- Thomas Edison -

Time to meet the Apache Cassandra NoSQL open-source distributed database management system. Cassandra is an absolutely essential tool for data scientists. There is virtually no company today concerned with large, active data sets which does not use Cassandra. The short list? Netflix, Twitter, Reddit, Cisco, OpenX, Digg, and CloudKick.

Cassandra offers all-important linear scalability and reliable fault-tolerance – the two key attributes of any platform required to manage mission-critical data. Per Apache: The platform offers optimal support for replicating across multiple data-centers; in this it allows lower latency and protection against regional outages. In short, Cassandra is a brilliantly efficient, non-traditional database that's been designated to easily scale up to massive data sets.

This free distribution from the Apache Software Foundation offers column indexes, log-structured updates, support for materialized views, and elegant built-in caching.

The database is completely fault tolerant. Cassandra automatically replicates (backs-up) data to multiple nodes or, if you prefer, to multiple data centers. Failing nodes can be replaced with absolutely no downtime interruption. This is, of course, a decentralized platform. Every node in a cluster is identical. There are no network bottlenecks, and no single points of failure.

At the same time, Cassandra is elastic. When new machines are added, read and write throughput increase linearly. There's no downtime, no interruption.

"We're consciously signaling that Cassandra is ready for mere mortals," said Jonathan Ellis, who is Apache's vice president in charge of the Cassandra project, jokingly referring to the amount administrative expertise needed to deploy previous versions of the software. "Dealing with very large amounts of data in real-time is a must for most businesses today. Cassandra accommodates high query volumes, provides enterprise-grade reliability, and scales easily to meet future growth requirements -while using fewer resources than traditional solutions."

Ellis says the difference between traditional databases like MySQL and Cassandra is the difference between analytic big data and real-time big data. He further notes that Hadoop itself is strictly an analytical system rather than a real time or transaction oriented system (ala Cassandra). Ellis: "On the real-time side, Cassandra's strongest competitors are probably Riak and HBase. Riak is backed by Basho, and I believe Cloudera supports HBase although it's not their focus. For analytics, everyone is standardizing on Hadoop, and there are a number of companies pushing that. ... "

Users find Cassandra indispensable.

"As the most-widely deployed mobile rich media advertising platform, Medialets uses Apache Cassandra for handling time series based logging from our production operations infrastructure," says Joe Stein, Chief Architect of Medialets. "We store contiguous counts for data points for each second, minute, hour, day, month so we can review trends over time as well as the current real time set of information for tens of thousands of data points.

Cassandra makes it possible for us to manage this intensive data set ... "

Matthew Conway, CTO of Backupify notes: "Apache Cassandra makes it possible for us to build a business around really high write loads in a scalable fashion without having to build and operate our own sharing layer. The [latest] release of Cassandra ... is an exciting milestone for the project and we look forward to exploring the new features and performance enhancements."

Hadoop

That's what's cool about working with computers. They don't argue, they remember everything, and they don't drink all your beer.

- Paul Leary -

High performance data analysis is a required competitive component, providing valuable insight into the behavior of customers, market trends, scientific data, business partners, and internal users. Explosive growth in the amount of data businesses must track has challenged legacy database platforms. New unstructured, text-centric, data sources, such as feeds from Facebook and Twitter do not fit into the structured data model. These unstructured datasets tend to be very big and difficult to work with. *They demand distributed (aka parallelized) processing.*

Hadoop, an open source software product, has emerged as the preferred solution for Big Data analytics. Because of its scalability, flexibility, and low cost, it has become the default choice for Web giants that are dealing with large-scale clickstream analysis and ad targeting scenarios. For these reasons and more, many industries who have been struggling with the limitations of traditional database platforms are now deploying Hadoop solutions in their data centers. (These industries are also looking for economy. According to some recent research from Infineta Systems, a WAN optimization startup, traditional data storage runs $5 per gigabyte, but storing the same data costs about 25 cents per gigabyte using Hadoop.)

Businesses are finding they need faster insight and deeper analysis of their data – slow performance equates to lost revenue. Hadoop – available in customized, proprietary versions from a range of vendors – provides a solid answer to this dilemma.

Hadoop is a free, Java-based programming framework that supports the processing of large data sets in a distributed computing environment. It is part of the Apache project sponsored by the Apache Software Foundation.

Hadoop was originally conceived on the basis of Google's *MapReduce*, in which an application is broken down into numerous small parts. Any of these parts (also called fragments or blocks) can be run on any node in the cluster. Hadoop makes it possible to run applications on systems with thousands of nodes involving thousands of terabytes.

A distributed file system (DFS) facilitates rapid data transfer rates among nodes and allows the system to continue operating uninterrupted in case of a node failure. The risk of catastrophic system failure is low, even if a significant number of nodes become inoperative.

The Hadoop framework is used by major players including Google, Yahoo and IBM, largely for applications involving search engines and advertising. The preferred operating systems are Windows and Linux but Hadoop can also work with BSD and OS X. (A bit of trivia: the name *Hadoop* was inspired by the name of a stuffed toy elephant belonging to a child of the framework's creator, Doug Cutting.)

Hadoop lies, invisibly, at the heart of many Internet services accessed daily by millions users around the world.

"Facebook uses Hadoop ... extensively to process large data sets," says Ashish Thusoo, Engineering Manager at Facebook. "This infrastructure is used for a variety of different jobs – including adhoc analysis, reporting, index generation and many others. We have one of the largest clusters with a total storage disk capacity of more than 20PB and with more than 23000 cores. We also use Hadoop and Scribe for log collection, bringing in more than 50TB of raw data per day. Hadoop has helped us scale with these tremendous data volumes."

"Hadoop is a key ingredient in allowing LinkedIn to build many of our most computationally difficult features, allowing us to harness our incredible data about the professional world for our users," comments Jay Kreps, LinkedIn's Principal Engineer.

Let's not forget Twitter. "Twitter's rapid growth means our users are generating more and more data each day. Hadoop enables us to store, process, and derive insights from our data in ways that wouldn't otherwise be possible. We are excited about the rate of progress that Hadoop is achieving, and will continue our contributions to its thriving open source community," notes Kevin Weil, Twitter's Analytics Lead.

Then we have eBay. During 2010, eBay erected a Hadoop cluster spanning 530 servers. By December of 2011, the cluster was five times that large, helping with everything from analyzing inventory data to building customer profiles using real-time online behavior. "We got tremendous value – tremendous value – out of it, so we've expanded to 2,500 nodes," says Bob Page, eBay's vice president of analytics. "Hadoop is an amazing technology stack. We now depend on it to run eBay."

*

"Hadoop has been called the next-generation platform for data processing because it offers low cost and the ultimate in scalability. But Hadoop is still immature and will need serious work by the community ... " writes *InformationWeek's* Doug Henschen. "Hadoop is at the center of this decade's Big Data revolution. This Java-based framework is actually a collection of software and subprojects for distributed processing of huge volumes of data. The core approach is MapReduce, a technique used to boil down tens or even hundreds of terabytes of Internet clickstream data, log-file data, network traffic streams, or masses of text from social network feeds."

We can trace the origins of Hadoop back to 2002. In that year, the Internet Archive's Doug Cutting together with a graduate student (Mike Cafarella from Washington State University) set out to build an open-source search engine they called *Nutch*. The idea was to be able to quickly crawl and process Internet data in what *was then* a great volume: several hundred million web pages. In retrospect, Nutch had a number of limitations which were bound to become crippling as the size and rate of data grew. First of all, it could only be run across a few machines at one time. As well, it was so unstable that human-eyes had to be on it 24-7 to make sure it didn't crash.

"I remember being quite proud of what we had been doing ..." notes Cafarella. "[But] then the Google File System paper came out [in October 2003] and I realized: 'Oh, that's a much better way of doing it ...'. Then, by the time we had a first working version, the MapReduce paper came out [in December 2004] and that seemed like a pretty good idea too."

Per Mike Olson: Hadoop's underlying technology "was invented by Google back in their earlier days so they could usefully index all the rich textural and structural information they were collecting, and then present meaningful and actionable results to users." Google's paper described a distributed scalable file system for very large, data-intensive, distributed applications. Requiring only highly-economical hardware, the system delivered robust fault-tolerance and very high-aggregate performance across many machines. Of most importance was the scalability: the capability to remain reliable as data grew in volume, and as the number of machines involved increased. At the time the paper was presented, the system was already in use at Google. The firm's largest cluster delivered many hundreds of terabytes of storage on thousands of disks scattered across thousands of machines. The paper was delivered at the 19 ACM Symposium on Operating System Principles held at Lake George, New York in October of 2003. The paper was authored by Sanjay Ghemawat, Howard Gobioff and Shun-Tak Leung.

Authored by Sanjay Ghemawat and Jeffrey Dean, Google's MapReduce paper described an elegant and radically-new programming model together with a superior implementation for creating and processing very large data sets. Within MapReduce, users defined map functions for the process of a key/value pair, this in turn generating a set of key/value pairs together with a reduce function that merged intermediate values merged with the same intermediate key.

"Programs written in this functional style are automatically parallelized and executed on a large cluster of commodity machines," wrote the authors. "The run-time system takes care of the details of partitioning the input data, scheduling the program's execution across a set of machines, handling machine failures, and managing the required inter-machine communication. This allows programmers without any experience with parallel and distributed systems to easily utilize the resources of a large distributed system. Our implementation of MapReduce runs on a large cluster of commodity machines and is highly scalable: a typical MapReduce computation processes many terabytes of data on thousands of machines. Programmers find the system easy to use: hundreds of MapReduce programs have been implemented and upwards of one thousand MapReduce jobs are executed on Google's clusters every day."

This paper was presented at OSDI'04: The Sixth Symposium on Operating System Design and Implementation, held in San Francisco in December of 2004.

MapReduce signaled a revolution. Looking back, Raymie Stata, former Yahoo Chief Technology Officer (CTO) and founder of the Hadoop startup VertiCloud, recalls MapReduce as a "fantastic kind of abstraction" over the heretofore common distributed computing procedures and algorithms. "Everyone had something that pretty much was like MapReduce because we were all solving the same problems. We were trying to handle literally billions of web pages on machines that are probably, if you go back and check, epsilon more powerful than today's cell phones. ... So there was no option but to latch hundreds to thousands of machines together to build the index. So it was out of desperation that MapReduce was invented."

In June 2014, ten years after the birth of MapReduce, Google execs at the Google I/O Developers Conference introduced Cloud Dataflow, which they said would replace MapReduce which, though robust in its prime, was nevertheless now "so 2004-ish." MapReduce is "batch oriented, when what you really need is a system that can handle both a large amount of data set aside for a scheduled batch process and one that can handle an ad hoc stream of unsorted data." So writes industry analyst Charles Babcock. With Cloud Dataflow deployed on Google Apps Engine or Compute Engine, data scientists can still do batch processing but also handle real-time streaming data. Thus does Google MapReduce go into retirement after worthy service, its work done.

But now, for our purposes, let's get back to the ancient days of 2004 and the revolution engendered by that newborn named *MapReduce*.

In the months following the presentation of the MapReduce paper, Cutting and Cafarella began work on the fundamental file systems and framework for processing that would eventually be called *Hadoop*. Importantly, the two pioneers worked using Java even though Google's MapReduce had been implemented using C++. In turn, they layed Nutch across the top of the framework.

Java, they correctly believed, offered the maximum portability they sought in their platform, with its handy "write once, run anywhere" adaptability and its convenient, rich array of class libraries. It should be noted, however, that in recent years some (though by no means *all*) technologists have questioned the wisdom of this move, as an optimized C++ implementation would run just as well while at the same time drawing less hardware capacity and related power. The trade-off, of course, would be ease of portability.

In any event, Hadoop was implemented in Java.

Cutting joined Yahoo as an engineer in 2006, by which time Carfella had become an associate professor at the University of Michigan. It was at this point that Carfella effectively removed himself from commercial Hadoop development in favor of focusing on academics. (He now jokes that his father calls him the "Pete Best'" of Big Data, recalling the original Beatles drummer who was left behind while the band skyrocketed to international fame. Carfella nevertheless continues to work on numerous Hadoop- and Big Data-related projects within the academic setting, and is more than content with his decision.)

At Yahoo, Cutting was charged with building open-source solutions based on the Google File System and MapReduce paradigms. It was at this point that Hadoop (which he'd recently named rather randomly and spontaneously after his young son's toy elephant) became an open-source project with the non-profit Apache Software Foundation. So far as Cutting was concerned, this seemed the ideal approach "because I was looking for more people to work on it, and people who had thousands of computers to run it on."

At this point, Hadoop - although showing great promise - was still quite an inefficient and clumsy implementation, by no means equipped to efficiently handle web-scale search, and Big Data was not yet even seriously envisioned as either a demand or a potential. Hortonworks CEO Eric Baldeschwieler: "The thing you gotta remember is at the time we started adopting it, the aspiration was definitely to rebuild Yahoo's web search infrastructure, but Hadoop only really worked on 5 to 20 nodes at that point, and it wasn't very performant, either."

Today, Raymie Stata talks about the "slow march" towards scalability. In fact, Hadoop development was nothing short of arduous, demanding invention and re-invention over and over again – constantly testing the ingenuity and engineering imagination of all who worked on it. "It was just an ongoing slog ... every factor of 2 or [even] 1.5 ... was serious engineering work."

Very slowly, as the Hadoop technology evolved over the course of several years, Yahoo rolled it out onto what engineers called a "research grid" for use by in-house practitioners of the craft which has since become known as "Data Science" – the mining of actionable business intelligence from constantly flowing and changing data. At first, Hadoop was engineered to extend across several dozen nodes, then eventually several hundred.

Per Baldschwieler: "This very quickly kind of exploded and became our core mission, because what happened is the data scientists not only got interesting research results — what we had anticipated — but they also prototyped new applications and demonstrated that those applications could substantially improve Yahoo's search relevance or Yahoo's advertising revenue."

Once Hadoop began demonstrating its tangible business viability (round about 2007), a certain level of formality was necessarily adopted around the platform. Yahoo was running most of its business (just about every click/batch process and nearly all the financial transactions) through Hadoop by 2008. Eventually Yahoo used Hadoop for the range of core tasks: hosting line-of-business applications, filtering for spam, and implementing user-specific personalization on individual Yahoo pages. All of this together demanded the creation of service level agreements, not to mention protocols to meet rigid Securities and Exchange Commission requirements with regard to security, seeing how Yahoo began to run all sponsored searches through Hadoop. It also demanded robust and constant growth. By 2011 - in which year Yahoo created its subsidiary firm HortonWorks and spun off all further Hadoop development - Yahoo's Hadoop infrastructure represented no less than 42,000 nodes and many hundreds of petabytes of storage. Concurrent with all this, Hadoop remained a vibrant open-source Apache project, with many individual developers coming up with a vast range of intriguing, robust innovations and solutions.

By far, Yahoo's most valuable contribution to the Hadoop platform was what Yahoo engineers dubbed the "Capacity Scheduler." This tool submits jobs in orderly queues, allocates a portion of resource capacity to each queue, allocates free resources to each queue beyond their total capacity, and assigns and enforces priority labels to the various queues.

Doug Cutting departed Yahoo in August of 2009 to join the start-up Cloudera, which had been founded by Christophe Bisciglia, Mike Olson, Jeff Hammerbacher and Amr Awadallah (the latter a former Yahoo engineering VP) one year earlier. Cloudera represented the very first commercial Hadoop enterprise, and it quickly became the port via which most corporate CIOs got their first look at the platform. Already a favorite of such early adopters as the engineers at Facebook, Hadoop soon became the dominant subject amid the tech industry's constant buzz and chatter. The IT and business press routinely sang the praises of its great promise, this revolutionary approach that offered not only massive economies of scale, but also invaluable real-time BI of a type, quality and timeliness that had not heretofore even been imagined, never mind achieved.

Today the Apache project continues to spur brilliant innovation, while at the same time a number of top software and database firms - among them Amazon, Microsoft and Oracle - offer their own highly-intuitive, emminently-efficient and easy-to-use proprietary commercial variations on the theme. Administering a massive distributed implementation such as Hadoop works with is an extremely complex operation. Most CIOs and corporate IT departments have neither the staff, staff-time or expertise to start from scratch and build a custom Hadoop application and system. Thus a range of vendors have stepped into the marketplace offering robust, easy-to-implement and manage turn-key Hadoop solutions for enterprises that want to get up and running as quickly, economically and safely as possible - without excessive costs and without unnecessary risk to data.

*

Beyond Hadoop, there are a number of other tools which are popular and vital to many data science efforts.

Scribe, Flume, and Kafka provide resources for the collection of streaming data. They garner data from many sources, aggregate that data, and then provide it to a database system such as Hadoop.

Languages for querying large non-relational data stores include Pig and Hive. While Pig is a data-oriented scripting tool, Hive is akin to SQL.

Meanwhile,Hbase, Voldemort, and Cassandra represent data stores that have been designed to handle very large datasets.

Orchestrating

Change

in the Workplace

Teamwork is the ability to work together toward a common vision. The ability to direct individual accomplishments toward organizational objectives. It is the fuel that allows common people to attain uncommon results.

- Andrew Carnegie -

Change is scary. Change is threatening. Change is annoying. Change is *work*.

But change is also exciting, invigorating, renewing, and refreshing. Change is the evolution, growth, and expansion of horizons. Change is the "creative destruction" of what has gone before to make way for better, smarter techniques, tools, and technologies. *New* thinking.

What's the biological alternative to evolution? You guessed it. Extinction.

In the workplace, change leads to organizational success and thereby organizational survival.

There's no more important skill than knowing how to innovate and manage this change.

Big Data and its compadre Data Science represent the most Draconian change to hit many a workplace in decades. In an age when information is everything, or very nearly everything, the flood of the constantly-flowing tsunami of of Big Data has drastically redefined the terrain of countless long-accepted business models and organizational practices.

Anciently established roles are thrown into states of flux; traditional chains of authority disrupted. Power changes hands. Veterans feel demeaned and become disgruntled. *Experience* – once respected – becomes a suspect thing: an artifact from a prior, antique time; a propeller in the era of the jet. The literati among us might be reminded of a line from W.B. Yeats: "Things fall apart; the centre cannot hold; Mere anarchy is loosed ..."

But the "centre" can and must hold. And anarchy is not an option.

It is the manager's job to make sure that uncertainty among veterans is minimized, disorder avoided, and the threat of chaos stopped in its tracks. It is the manager's job to make sure that new shoes do not unduly step on old toes. It is the manager's job to take a situation ripe with potential for rivalries and transform it into an opportunity for team-building and for the building of a more sustainable, effective, and profitable culture.

It is important that all players understand and buy into the vision of a data-driven workplace: a workplace where professionals acquire, interpret, and leverage data in order to maximize efficiencies, iterate and create new products and service initiatives, and otherwise successfully navigate the emerging and constantly changing competitive landscape.

It is also important that managers understand the importance of the "democratization" of data. Granular and key metrics data, once defined, should be shared by all decision makers in the organization, not just amongst the data science team. The data science team should propose conclusions, but not impose them. Conclusions should be jointly arrived at, and should be the result of merging data science results with the experiential knowledge of line-managers and other key professionals. As well, all appropriate professionals – not just data scientists – should be armed with the tools, training, and permissions to make their own queries into the firm's data store, whether this be Hadoop-based or otherwise configured.

Throughout all, the importance of cooperation and coordination between traditional and non-traditional players cannot be overemphasized. The most important task the manager faces is to marshall and orchestrate this cooperation and coordination, and make it blossom into productive results for the entire enterprise.

Vince Lombardi commented: *Individual commitment to a group effort – that is what makes a team work, a company work, a society work, a civilization work.*

The "Quants" with all their metrics hold a key position on your team, but not the only position. It is important that the players in the field respect the work of the pitcher, but equally important that they know the pitcher respects them and understands their role as being vital. Especially since several of the outfielders were once pitchers.

About

the Authors

Lars Nielsen's bestselling books include *Computing: A Business History, Unicorns Among Us: Understanding the High Priests of Data Science,* and *Dark Data and Dark Social: The Promising Problem Children of Data Science.*

Noreen Burlingame is a programmer/consultant and the co-author of *A Simple Introduction to Data Science.*

Robert Masters is an independent programmer, systems analyst, and technical writer.

Also of Interest …

www.ingramcontent.com/pod-product-compliance
Lightning Source LLC
Chambersburg PA
CBHW071004050326
40689CB00014B/3480

* 9 7 8 0 6 9 2 6 6 2 0 9 0 *